THE
MELTING
POINT

THE
MELTING
POINT

HOW TO STAY COOL AND SUSTAIN
WORLD-CLASS
BUSINESS PERFORMANCE

Dr. Christian Marcolli

urbanepublications.com

First published in Great Britain in 2017 by Urbane Publications Ltd
Suite 3, Brown Europe House, 33/34 Gleaming Wood Drive, Chatham, Kent ME5 8RZ
Copyright © Christian Marcolli, 2017

A CIP catalogue record for this book is available from the British Library.

ISBN 978-1-911129-24-0
MOBI 978-1-911129-26-4
EPUB 978-1-911129-25-7

Design and Typeset by Julie Martin
Cover by Julie Martin

Printed and bound by CPI Group (UK) Ltd, Croydon, CR0 4YY

urbanepublications.com

I dedicate this book to all the executives and leaders who don't just aspire to continuously develop themselves, but who put in the hard work day in and day out to reach their absolute personal best. Your commitment is a huge inspiration to me. Working with you is a privilege.

CONTENTS

FOREWORD

Top corporate performers have really intense lives. Their jobs are highly complex and constantly changing, and they must stay on top of ever increasing demands at work and at home. Intensity can be exciting, but too much can quickly wear us down. The challenge, it seems, is how to manage it. Christian Marcolli, drawing on his extensive experience working with executives and athletes – such as Roger Federer – and other extremely high performers, provides us with a comprehensive look at how we can better understand, and manage, intensity and reach our personal best.

Christian explores the many facets of high-pressure environments and how they impact us personally and professionally. He also makes the case, using some of his former clients, about how managing our stress levels can change the trajectory of our careers and our lives. The story is quite compelling.

But Christian doesn't stop there. He then lays out the various stages that we go through in our careers, and explains the specific challenges we are prone to face at particularly vulnerable moments. Most important of all, Marcolli shows us how we can avoid that stress trap, and get to a place in our careers where instead of burning out, we can enter a period of heightened performance, even playfulness. I don't know a leader of any kind who wouldn't benefit greatly from reaching that level.

The Melting Point is not a quick fix tool for making our lives carefree and easy. It is a comprehensive, thorough and multi-faceted look at a subject that has never been more relevant than it is today.

Patrick Lencioni
Author of *The Five Dysfunctions of a Team* and *The Advantage*

INTRODUCTION

Let's begin with a question: How busy are you? Take a precious moment to consider that question fully. Go on, put the phone down, close the email, and spend a minute thinking about your average day or week. I suspect you are very busy, and not simply with the pressures of a challenging job. I am sure that you are also trying to achieve a positive integration of your work and home life to maximize your overall life experience. Whether you are a business leader, an executive, a top corporate performer or an ambitious manager, I suspect you're putting in 60-hour weeks (or more), continually prioritizing and reprioritizing tasks and deadlines. The question is this (and it's one we should all consider): is there a point on that high-pressure journey where you start to flame out? Will your mind (and body) turn and yell, "No more!", and if it does, what will the impact be on your life both at work and at home? Most importantly, how will you cope?

This point when things start to collapse from within is represented by the book's title "The Melting Point". It refers to the critical psychological threshold that all of us face when placed under massive stress and pressure. It is the moment where – and when – we lose our cool. It applies primarily to business leaders, executives and corporate performers – but not exclusively. The Melting

Point also applies to elite athletes and coaches, as well as to those operating in highly-pressured environments, from top-performing artists and musicians, to politicians and military personnel.

We have reached the Melting Point when we no longer fully control our thinking, our emotions and our behaviors, in a positive and impactful way. We start to internally derail, to display dysfunctional behaviors and are likely to make mistakes. It becomes very clear that we are far from being at our personal best; the errors – and the stress that caused them – may even force us to walk away, because the pressure seems to be simply too much to bear. Ultimately, reaching the Melting Point may stop us from achieving our key goals and ambitions.

If that all sounds very dramatic and negative, take heart. Because there is an effective way to not just to cope with the Melting Point, but to spot the warning signs long before you start to 'melt'. With that awareness, you can learn ways to raise your Melting Point and be at your best during intense and challenging times.

You've probably heard people claim that they "thrive under pressure". You can too. You can achieve sustainable world-class performance in business by raising your Melting Point, and master the enormous pressures of today's demanding business environment, while staying in control. You'll be able to maintain a winning edge in your career, lead your teams proactively and effectively, and benefit your organization for the long-term. And the icing on the cake? It will give you the means to develop not just an enjoyable career, but a fulfilling life.

Before we begin to explore the actual specifics of the Melting Point for you individually – what it is, how you recognize it, how you manage it in the short-term and how you further exploit it positively – we need to take a look more broadly at aspects of pressure and where the concept of the Melting Point comes from.

At different times in a career, we are able to achieve the highest levels of performance during certain episodes or phases. The true skill is maintaining those levels consistently, without any detrimental effects on our productivity or sacrifice of our physical and mental wellbeing. Sustaining a high level of performance every day, week after week, in changing environments that are highly competitive, can be complex and very stressful. So raising your Melting Point is one of the most – if not

THE most – critical factors in sustaining world-class performance.

We have all heard accounts of people failing under pressure: the tennis player who throws away a match-winning tie-break; or the executive who makes irrational decisions that ultimately destroy a company. Maybe you have seen it with a colleague, or even approached that point yourself – that one moment when it all gets too much, when it all threatens to come crashing down. In contrast, those who excel consistently don't let the pressure get in their way. They're adaptable, they deal with their emotions and move on to an even higher level of performance. You can also learn how to do that. Instead of letting your passion and ambition become a burden, learn to use them in a controlled and positive way.

Many of us deal with these aspects of sustainable top performance in isolation. How should we react, respond and adapt to high-pressure situations? Why is it that some colleagues clearly perform better than others? Why do some show what they can really do in challenging situations, while others lose their edge on the big stage? Why do some people recover faster from setbacks than others? What are the keys to sustaining high performance, especially under pressure or in times of change?

Ultimately, you can only achieve the top level of performance on an ongoing basis if you execute in a playful, enjoyable way. My own work with sports' superstars and corporate clients has always been targeted to achieve sustainable top performance in this manner. At their best, these top performers are an inspiration to other people. You can also attain this same level by embracing a specific developmental journey – Executive Performance Transformation. Over the following chapters, you will be introduced to the stages of this transformation, allowing you to easily assess your own performance level and develop a plan to reach greater heights.

This book is built upon an inspirational series of interviews with top business leaders, executives, corporate performers and ambitious managers. The guidance it contains will help you raise your own Melting Point, and develop the skillset required to not only manage but excel in pressure situations. The concepts are brought to life with a unique selection of original case studies and real-life experiences from a range of actual clients. Confidentiality is obviously essential, so the case examples are composites of real-life stories from client sessions and during corporate programs with leadership teams, and are based on the real challenges faced by the leaders of some of the world's most successful companies. They give a powerful example of how these determined individuals have been able to face their personal challenges and transform their lives, experiencing Executive Performance Transformation with long-lasting benefits.

The purpose in writing this book is to provide you with the insights and tools to raise your own Melting Point, delivering sustainable world-class performance in difficult, changing conditions, in a playful way. Mastering your own Melting Point isn't just about overcoming challenging situations and coping with pressure. It is more than that. By mastering the concepts in this book, you will not only maximize your performance and your business results, but also be at your most effective and inspiring as a leader. And – equally important – you will enjoy the intensity of the of high-pressure business environment. You deserve to succeed, so let's show you how!

CHAPTER 1

WHAT IT TAKES TO BECOME WORLD CLASS

This book is focused firmly on the world of business performance. But in this opening chapter, I want to share some relevant insights about the development of world-class performance in a similarly intense field – the world of elite, professional sport.

There are many positive analogies to be drawn between business and sport, and my own background as both a professional athlete and performance psychologist for some of the world's best athletes, coaches and leaders, has given me a unique insight into the challenges faced by them all. So let's begin by introducing the concept of the Melting Point with some examples drawn from the world of elite sport.

GETTING TO THE TOP

I want to challenge the notion that great performers are born rather than made. There is a common misconception that some people are simply born with an exceptional talent – and that these naturally gifted people are somehow preordained to become great in their field. This is a broken concept. Why? Because it makes us believe that there are some people who achieve great things effortlessly.

Often such people are characterized as "born champions", and their success is attributed to God-given talent or exceptional genes. But in fact that is rarely, if ever, the main reason for their success.

People only ever achieve true success when they combine their skill with their unique mental approach. These factors, in turn, are invariably developed through a combination of innate aptitude and hard work. Aptitude matters, and yet it's mostly hard work that moves the needle. It requires focusing on the right things, at the right time in their career, and with the support of the right people.

However, this brings its own set of challenges.

PRACTICE MAKES PERFECT

We have all heard the old adage "practice makes perfect". And some studies suggest that it takes 10,000 hours of deliberate practice to become an expert in a field – whether it is sport, music or another skill. This equates to 20 hours of practice a week, for 50 weeks a year, over the course of 10 years.

In most areas of expertise, individuals embark on a

program of deliberate practice to optimize improvement, and differences in individuals' results, even among elite performers, are closely related to the amount of deliberate practice they have clocked up. This fact alone largely explodes the myth of natural ability being the key driver of success. It shows us that many characteristics often thought to reflect innate talent are actually the result of intense practice over many years.

Not all forms of practice are, however, equal in terms of focus or effectiveness. The most effective practice not only involves many repetitions over a lengthy period, but needs to be enhanced by "fine tuning" the right behaviors based on measurement and analysis.

Many successful performers that have been labeled as naturally gifted have practiced for *thousands* of hours to reach their goals, often using leading edge technology and benefiting from the help of expert coaches.

In the world of sport, for example, the idea that elite athletes are simply the lucky recipients of the right genes is clearly nonsense. People with flair, flamboyance, elegance and seemingly effortless ability have also had to work extremely hard. My point is illustrated by an anecdote involving the great South African golfer Gary Player. When Gary holed his ball with a perfectly aimed chip from far off the green, his playing partner accused him of being simply lucky. Player wryly responded, "The funny thing is, the more I practice, the luckier I get."

Both empirical research and my own experience coaching individuals and corporate clients show that achieving world-class performance – as an athlete, coach, a businessperson, or in any other specialty – does not just happen because of natural talent. They have become true experts in their field by building up their mastery with focused development. However, in addition to "the hard work", there are necessary components that stand out with exceptional performers.

It boils down to more recognizable traits. The first is their *passion*. It is absolutely necessary that high performing individuals have a strong passion for their area of achievement. Passion is the fuel for their journey to success – and they need a full tank of it to drive them from the start of that journey to the finish.

The second element is their *adaptability*. This dictates the degree to which individuals can engage with and process high quality information and bring it to bear effectively on their behaviors.

Adaptability is not simply an intellectual skill. Many people can recognize faults and weaknesses in their performance and understand the behavioral changes they need to make to correct them, but they often fail to implement such changes effectively. There is a strong tendency in certain circumstances, and especially when under pressure, to fall back into old patterns and habits or to forget to apply new learning.

The third thing is how 'cool' they are when they execute their performance under difficult conditions. The best performers can excel in very highly-charged, critical moments, and don't allow anxiety and nervousness to get in the way of being at their best.

Teach Me Patience, Now! and *More Life, Please!*, explored in depth the critical role passion plays in one's professional and personal life. And *The Melting Point* specifically focuses on the one critical factor for sustainable world-class performance that has been generally overlooked: staying cool. You will see that the ability to remain cool and raise your Melting Point has profound benefits.

> **The three most important components for exceptional performance**
>
> 1. **Passion**
>
> 2. **Adaptability**
>
> 3. **Coolness**

CHANGING ATTITUDE AND BEHAVIORS

Often the ability to remain cool and to avoid melting down is aligned with experience. It is assumed that people will go through a series of situational events throughout their career, they learn from them, and this accumulation of experience will automatically increase their Melting Point. Actually, most people go through such events without much effect. On the other hand, some of the most successful athletes touch great heights of performance without having had the opportunity to gain a lot of experience. So the Melting Point is not raised by experience *per se*. It is raised by changed attitude and behaviors, fundamentally based on Personal Leadership

Excellence (more on this in the final chapter of the book). Crucially, however, with focus and effort, raising one's Melting Point can absolutely be learned.

COMMON DEVELOPMENT PATTERNS

We have established that top performers invariably have innate aptitude and work hard to develop their talent with expert input from their coaches. They also have the three recognizable traits – passion, adaptability, and coolness. But it is also important to recognize that top performers appear to make a number of key transitions as they develop.

There is a critical transition to make at the highest level: moving from obsession with a chosen specialty to transforming that energy into success. In professional sports, the first victory at the top level for an athlete is a huge step, placing them in a highly exclusive circle of winners.

Winning brings one major change in top athletes: it makes them relaxed in their mastery. They become so comfortable in their level of performance that they make it appear effortless. Ultimately, they can even become playful, often experimenting with new techniques and enjoying their sport as much as they did when they were first introduced to it.

These developmental stages have been evident in much of my work with successful performers over the last 20 years. No doubt there are a few cases where sporting champions have taken an unconventional path, perhaps starting later in life or missing out on coaching or practice at some stages. However, a close look at their careers will still reveal the key elements – and what is truly extraordinary is the way they have managed to achieve their top position by overcoming such challenges.

THE MENTAL GAME: INSIGHTS FROM WORKING WITH SPORT CHAMPIONS

I have been privileged to work directly with a number of exceptional athletes who were keen to learn how performance psychology could help them reach the top of their game – and stay there.

Among these clients was Roger Federer, the tennis champion. At the time of our collaboration, he was early in his professional career and was looking to take his game to another level. He was coming to the end of his time as a junior and was making the transition to the ATP Tour, facing the challenges of life on the professional circuit.

Although many of the athletes that I coach are superb at their sport, I realized that practice, while important, isn't the only key factor behind their success. For the truly exceptional athletes, the ability to perform at such a high level even at a young age suggests they had "something" beyond the established theory that the amount of practice hours is the key determinant of success.

For example, an extraordinarily successful player in their late teens wouldn't have been able to accrue the same number of hours of deliberate practice as players 5 or 10 years older. There must be something else beyond the sheer number of hours of practice that a young player invests in their skills, even if that practice was highly focused and scientifically optimized for its effectiveness.

So, what was the biggest difference between a champion like Roger and the many other very fine tennis players performing on the tour? The answer is not necessarily athleticism alone. Nor, in my view, is it natural ability or technical prowess. Yes, many sports stars have all of these attributes in abundance, giving them an equal opportunity to reach great heights.

In addition to an enormous passion for the sport, however, what makes such a champion so special is twofold: firstly, they are extremely adaptable. By this I mean they can very easily absorb new information and adapt their behavior incredibly quickly, adopting improvements and letting go of dysfunctional patterns. The result is that they can change the outcomes and reach new performance heights in relatively short periods of time.

Secondly, they manage to develop an extraordinarily high Melting Point relatively early in their career through a dedicated focus on their mental game.

As it has been constantly noted in the media, Roger's ability to perform under massive pressure has provided a crucial advantage. Or, in other words: Roger's Melting Point over time became so high that almost every other player in the world started to "melt" before he did. He was able to play with the same intense focus, and to the same extraordinarily high level, regardless of the situation and the pressure. In fact, the more important the matches were, the more playful he appeared. His opponents knew it and, because they knew it, he had a very special advantage. At his peak he acquired an aura of near invincibility. And as his recent Australian Open victory proves that advantage is still very much in evidence.

Another example is the top skier Dominique Gisin, who overcame an incredible number of major setbacks to become an Olympic Champion. Dominique had multiple knee surgeries as a teenager – which is the time when an athlete develops the most – and as a result she was only able to compete in two official races between the ages of 15 and 18. During the same time period, her rivals clocked up over 110 races. There was no way she could ever overcome such a huge shortfall in experience. In addition, she had missed out on thousands of hours of practice, leaving her at a seemingly impossible disadvantage.

Dominique had to find another way to compete effectively at the highest level in her sport. My role was to prepare her to overcome these obstacles, despite the fact that she couldn't build up her robustness through lots of races and hours of practice on the slopes.

The objective was to raise her Melting Point so she was able to perform at her best under very difficult circumstances – as a result her performance on the slope would feel natural to her, even though she had much less opportunity to build experience via real races. Dominique's immense challenge throughout her whole career – besides finding the energy and determination to go through multiple rehabilitations after injury – was to find the exact right intensity to push herself and perform at her limit. With less opportunities to race, her strong desire to succeed meant that she could at times push too hard, performing beyond her limits and with a loss of control, leading to dangerous crashes. She kept her motivation up by constantly striving for her full potential, learning to make steady progress step-by-step, even if they were small steps. She was able to cool down the heat by adapting the speed. Ultimately, at the age of 28, she was able to perform at the highest level to win the gold medal at the Olympic Games – the result of incredible passion, learning agility, and the ability to stay cool during the greatest pressure of her career.

Similar outcomes can be seen with some top sports coaches, transformations that allow them to deliver outstanding coaching performance on a sustainable level. Their strong and consistent performance is also based on their passion, adaptability and coolness under pressure. They make their impact in a playful way, like Severin Lüthi, Roger Federer's longstanding tennis coach and Captain of the Swiss Team that won the World Cup of Tennis, the Davis Cup.

Severin reflects here on what it takes to be (and stay) world-class in the world of tennis:

BECOMING AND STAYING WORLD CLASS

One thing that I am certain about, with the players I coach, is that very often the work involves focusing on someone's personality more than their technique. Especially at the top level, you really need to improve every day. If you are not improving, then your level is effectively going down because there are enough opponents who are working their hardest to improve. So especially when the players are young, you need to specifically work on their character to prepare them for tough times. At first, it is hard for them to understand that they have to invest beyond normal training. They need to realize that they must invest in their career, and specifically in the development of their character as well.

It is not all that different for coaches. If you as a coach want to make it to the top and stay there, you need to be able to make improvements. You need to reflect about what you can do better because perhaps what is a good solution today is not the right solution in two months or a year. You must always try to approach the problem differently, to not be afraid to adapt even when things have proved to work in the past. For example, it is very interesting for me to hear what works well in other sports, and to get familiar with different approaches outside of tennis. The solutions may not be exactly the same, but these ideas are very inspiring.

Personally, I can be strong-willed, and I recognize that I am not always a guy who likes to listen to others. However, I have learned the value of being open to input and criticism. It has helped me to find a very compelling approach towards my work at the highest level: I look at it in a similar way as the players look at playing the game. I realized that passion and willpower alone wouldn't make me a great coach. In order to stay at the top of the game over many years, I had to find my own approach with similar components to the players at the highest level.

So instead of doing the job of a coach, I look at it as 'playing my best coaching game'. Christian has helped me to develop this attitude and with that, raise my own Melting Point.

Severin Lüthi, one of the most successful Coaches in the history of Tennis, on coaching players to win multiple Grand Slam titles, Olympic Medals and the World Cup of Tennis, the Davis Cup.

Obviously coaching top athletes is high pressure and extremely demanding. Key to Severin's success as a coach is his own adaptability, being open to feedback and able to take on new information and techniques to constantly evolve his own "coaching game".

DEVELOPING WORLD-CLASS PERFORMANCE IN BUSINESS

So far in this book, we have looked in some detail at what it means to develop to a world-class performance level in the arena of sport. Of course, high performance in sport and business are not exactly the same. For a start, we don't generally introduce our children to the world of office work at a tender young age, in the same way that we might kick a ball around with them, take them to the local tennis courts or encourage them onto the ski slopes.

There are however clear parallels with sport. As corporate performers reach the top levels of their field, the best leaders must ignore the enormity of their challenge and concentrate instead on what they need to do to perform to their highest standard day-in and day-out. For business leaders, the ability to move their Melting Point offers the opportunity to shift positively from a short-term, "firefighting" mindset to a much more strategic, planned and composed approach to the demands of corporate life.

Later in the book, executives describe what pain points they have encountered and how they have been able to address them by developing Personal Leadership

Excellence, avoiding career stall, maintaining their composure and momentum – and transitioning successfully to the next stage of their executive performance, achieving greater heights on a sustainable level.

However, we first need to understand why life has become so tough for business leaders in today's challenging workplace.

CHAPTER 2

FEELING THE HEAT

For top business performers, managing pressure has always been demanding. But in today's highly competitive, fast-moving, globalized business environment, it is harder than ever. In this technology-driven, "always-on" world, how do you plan your business life and achieve sustainable high performance, while also creating harmony and contentment at home?

The challenges for many corporate executives include reduced budgets, work overload, increased complexity, uncertainty and greater ambiguity. In such demanding conditions, many find themselves constantly at their limit, often being physically stressed, mentally exhausted, and emotionally drained – less than ideal conditions for being consistently at their personal best. In addition, many suffer job insecurity and risk setbacks such as career burnout and fractured personal relationships.

Perhaps none of this applies to you? You may be someone who has somehow managed to attain that rare integration of success in your field and happiness at home. Does your workforce try to emulate you, do your peers admire you, does your boss rely on you, and does your family adore you? More importantly, have you achieved a feeling of inner peace, with a true deeper purpose for your actions? If the answer is yes to all of the above, I congratulate you, you are indeed a star – and one that is seen all too rarely. And I'd like to include your case study in the next book!

In my experience, however, many of today's business decision-makers – despite often performing well and climbing the corporate ladder – are close to the limits of what they can endure. Their energy is depleted and therefore the likelihood of sustaining their success diminishes. They are often close to their personal Melting Point and their careers are vulnerable to stalling.

They desperately need a performance transformation, a shift from merely trying to survive, to enjoying a successful and satisfying life journey. They need to regain perspective, get back to physical fitness, create mental resilience and restore their emotional stability based on a good sense of purpose and deeper meaning.

They need this performance transformation for the benefit of their careers, to remain inspirational in their professional roles, and to continue their rise through the corporate hierarchy.

They need it so that they can inspire and lead their teams effectively.

They need it for their own personal health, happiness and security.

And, not least, their businesses need them to achieve this performance transformation, for the sake of corporate competitiveness and, ultimately, sustainable bottom line results – especially in times of change. And change is omnipresent.

TECHNOLOGY INCREASING THE PACE OF CHANGE

Just look at the way technology has changed our lives over the last few decades. We live in a data-driven world, and the impact on our work lives is immeasurable.

It is inconceivable that we could live without "always on" technology. Just-in-time processes have revolutionized the manufacturing and retail sectors; email and instant messaging have speeded up the way we deal with colleagues and organize our schedules. Social media brings us in touch with more people, news and commentary than an individual can reasonably process.

We're clicking our way to a huge online marketplace, an ever-expanding social network and a more fast-paced, streamlined work environment, with business colleagues in another continent as accessible as those in the office next door.

The explosion of high-speed internet and mobile technology have given us the flexibility to work remotely and complete important tasks while traveling. But our devices tether us to our workplaces and our working environment has become fluid: we're telecommuting more than ever, we work when we're travelling, we work when we're at home, and we're always connected.

The lines between work and home, therefore, are becoming blurred. Research points to a direct correlation between mobile communication and workplace pressure, because of the ubiquitous nature of mobile devices. The technology's flexibility is undeniable – we are freed up to work at home, and we can now be productive wherever we happen to be. And by association we are expected to be productive wherever we happen to be. We are not switching off, and that lack of downtime contributes to elevated levels of anxiety and stress.

In today's supercharged world, you're likely to be consulted instantly whenever something needs your input, however large or small, work days or weekends. Add to that the constant stream of emails flooding your inbox every day – many irrelevant, but just as many requesting your action or decision – and you have a recipe for interruption, irritation and inefficiency. Such overload is bound to clutter your mind and can leave you frustrated and stressed, less able either to concentrate fully on the key performance areas of your job, or relax completely when you are away from work.

OUR COMPLEX, GLOBAL WORKPLACE

Globalization, according to *The Economist*, is, "the more or less simultaneous marketing and sale of identical goods and services around the world". It is why the familiar brands we have always known at home are now seen all over the world. Companies can establish offices across the globe, attracting clients and consumers they wouldn't have dreamed of decades ago. Emerging markets have increased competition between, and demand for, consumer goods, services and technologies.

Although opportunities abound for organizations in this diverse global marketplace, the subsequent complexity of the systems they need in order to operate can be hugely challenging to manage, and this in turn places pressure on individual executives. Developing processes, adapting products, managing distribution channels, respecting cultural differences, understanding legal and regulatory issues – any one of these can lead to too much organizational and personal vulnerability.

Staying ahead of the competition, mitigating risk, dealing with legal and regulatory pressures, managing a diverse workforce and working in different time zones – you have your work cut out for you in today's interconnected world!

Many executives cope with global competition by working their hardest to create a high-performance culture in their organization. This means that there are constantly more tasks to be accomplished than can ever be possible within a limited timeframe and resources. Business is relentless, twenty-four hours a day, across all time zones.

As a mid- and long-term consequence, organizations will renew themselves on a regular basis to stay competitive, seeking gains in efficiency and effectiveness. On an individual level, however, it puts key performers under constant stress, facing more targets than they can possibly deliver upon.

RISKY BUSINESS

A variety of risks are causing multiple concerns to industry leaders, including fiscal crises in key economies, a global governance failure and the collapse of banking institutions. And although the risks are diverse – ranging from water and climate change to political, social and financial instability – they are also interconnected, and have impacts that need managing across the board.

Supply chain risk is just one major area of concern for many global brands. Take, for example, a natural event such as a volcanic eruption, which led to severe disruption in the airline industry; or earthquakes and tsunamis, causing supply chain chaos for global manufacturers of electronics and automobiles. When components from Asia, for example, become temporarily unavailable, entire production lines on the other side of the world can grind to a halt.

As there is no global authority to control the global risks businesses face, so it falls upon organizations and individual leaders to build resilience. It all adds up to significant stress for busy executives who really do have the cares of the world on their shoulders.

The global financial crisis and financial scandals have hardened the attitude of regulators, shareholders and the public towards business leaders. A repeat of the corporate sins of the past won't be tolerated – and business leaders are under intense pressure and scrutiny to ensure they don't re-occur. Their exposure to lawsuits is on the increase, as regulators and shareholders focus on high standards of corporate governance and look to hold individual executives personally liable for failures.

The number of claims brought against company directors and officers has risen steeply in recent years and has created heightened exposure for those in multinational companies. Shareholders worldwide are looking to hold individual decision-makers legally accountable, trying to bring directors to account for losses suffered as a result of misrepresentations to financial markets.

To be found at fault carries the threat of both financial and non-monetary penalties – ranging from settlements and fines to ignominious departure, disqualification and even imprisonment.

COPING WITH MENTAL PRESSURE

We all have mental health, just as we all have physical health, and both can change during the course of our lives. Like our bodies, our minds can become unwell.

You only have to witness the growth of the spa sector, and the rise of courses in contemplative skills such as meditation, yoga and mindfulness, to see that many of us are craving respite and peace of mind as an essential antidote to today's working environment. Paying attention to the present is a popular trend, because it helps to rewire our brains in a turbulent world.

All too often people are afraid to talk about their mental and emotional problems because they fear disclosure will affect their jobs, reputation or relationships. For high-flying executives, expectations of their resilience are high, and they also have so much to lose.

From the employer's point of view, it is yet another challenging issue to face, while for the employees themselves, the stigma surrounding mental health still makes it hard for them to be open and honest.

The intense workplace isn't going to go away, and leaders need to understand the impact of this - on themselves, on their teams and on their organizations.

FACING THE CHALLENGE

So, very often, today's business executives have too much on their plate. To continue the metaphor, all too often the pace, complexity and uncertainty of today's business environment makes this particular meal unpalatable and even indigestible at times.

The effects of this challenge, if left unaddressed, are potentially far-reaching. Individuals will struggle to maintain the high level of performance through which they reached their influential position in the first place. There is a high risk that they will tire (first mentally, but then also physically), their motivation will drop, and their performance in their key role will fall away. In the most serious cases, they will potentially reach burnout, not only damaging their career, but their health and personal relationships too.

For the organization, this is not the end of the story. In large global organizations leaders can ultimately be responsible for hundreds or thousands of employees who are often struggling with these same challenges too, and are therefore more in need of leadership than ever before.

What will happen to the employees and teams if its leaders are not performing? The answer is all too clear: they will be asked to implement incorrect strategies (based on poor decisions), their motivation and engagement will be undermined, loyalty will dissipate, team performance will be eroded and, ultimately, valuable people will leave.

The impact on the organization of even one senior executive underperforming can be extensive, perhaps denting the profitability of a business division or the efficiency of a specialist function. But imagine this impact multiplied many times, as numerous executives lose their winning edge.

This isn't difficult to envisage in today's over-stretched corporations, and the impact would seriously reduce bottom line profits, shareholder value and investor confidence. Ultimately, the whole future of the corporation could be at stake.

The challenge facing individual executives, their teams and their businesses is clear for all to see: how can they perform consistently at their best in today's highly pressured, complex and ever-changing environment? One of the best places to start is on an individual level – and there is much we can do to help ourselves. It is about embracing Executive Performance Transformation.

CHAPTER 3

THE EXECUTIVE
PERFORMANCE
TRANSFORMATION

Sustaining top performance in business is not something that is achieved overnight. Rather, it happens by applying specific critical elements across an individual's career path as they strive to improve and advance in an ever-changing professional environment. It can be thought of as an **executive performance transformation** which follows a specific development path that involves learning and gaining mastery at each step in the process.

The development path to perform at the highest level in business can be segmented into four psychological stages. Over time, an individual's career follows a certain trajectory where they move through various stages: from **drawn in** to **obsessed**, then to a stage called **ready for success.** In an ideal case, they reach the ultimate stage of being **playful**.

The Four Stages of Executive Performance Transformation

1. Drawn in
2. Obsessed
3. Ready for success
4. Playful

While moving through these stages, an individual's level of performance continues to increase. Very often, however, situational factors can get in the way. Individuals on this journey can be derailed and reach a critical point of near meltdown.

As noted previously, the speed of this performance transformation will depend on the degree of passion the individual has for their work and role, their degree of

The Executive Performance Transformation

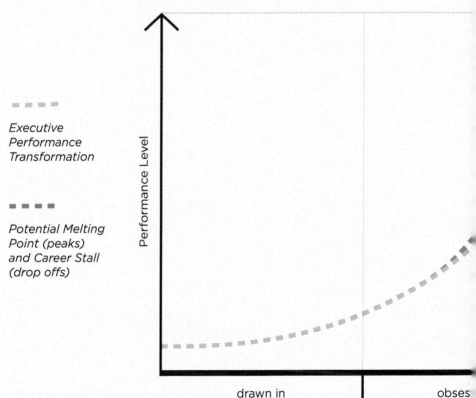

Executive Performance Transformation

Potential Melting Point (peaks) and Career Stall (drop offs)

Performance Level

drawn in

obses

adaptability, and how effective they are at developing their level of coolness.

In order to do so, individuals need to be exposed to challenges and stress. Let me be very clear: Growth never happens when there is only a comfort zone.

The following model illustrates the Executive Performance Transformation:

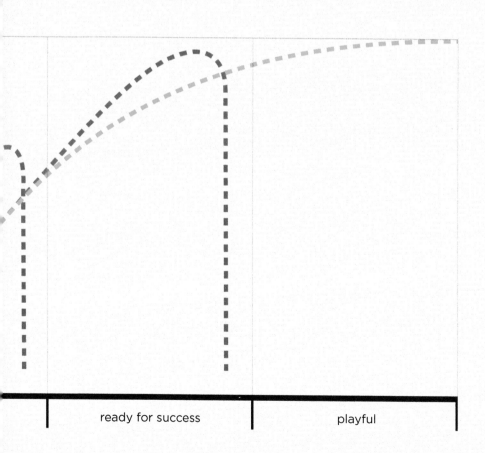

| ready for success | playful |

Drawn in

The first stage can be best described as drawn in. Whether that discipline is management, economics, marketing, law, HR, engineering or some other specialty, executives experience a connection described as, "I really like what I do", "the activities resonate with me" and "I find my role very fulfilling". At this stage, the performance is very engaged and enthusiastic. Because corporate performers are drawn in, they very naturally become experimental within their discipline, wanting to explore more. Doing really well is the main focus here, but success is not the only factor. In fact, the most important aspect is finding the work a great experience. There is not only a sense of accomplishment, but also the feeling of becoming competent in a specific area. Most often, it goes hand in hand with positive feedback. This increases the positive experience and the motivation. During this phase, there is very little risk of career stall.

From drawn in to obsessed

Depending on the ambition of the individual, the passion for the specific work will now lead to a highly-determined commitment to improve and grow. To master all of the challenges they face in the current position, the professionals become highly intense and focused – even obsessed. They allow it to dominate their lives, working extremely hard, and undertaking development programs to embark on a steep learning curve. They have the inner desire to do everything really well themselves, become better, perhaps aspiring even to become the best in their field. Large organizations make an effort to identify such individuals, often in the context of internal top talent programs, and offer additional development activities that accelerate their corporate experience, knowledge and skills. This is a very intense stage where corporate performers usually make the most significant progress in their performance level, but also where they usually reach their limits regarding how much they can take on and deliver – and potentially even negatively impacting their performance.

From obsessed to ready for success

As their expertise grows through increasing experience, corporate top performers enter their third stage – "ready for success". The move from the previous stage to this next one is subtle, with no sharp dividing lines between them, but in this phase they know more, achieve more and are just one step away from true mastery. Typically, formal professional development or coaching also plays a role. It is about preparing for true success, although notably, not all individuals can advance beyond obsessed to this next stage.

For many executives, leaders and corporate performers, this performance transition is difficult to achieve. A large number are *not* making this transition properly, and end up constantly delivering their performance in an obsessed way. This results in tension and is not enjoyable for anyone – not for themselves, nor for their teams and organization, and definitely not for their family and friends at home. This may lead to major frustration.

This transition really only happens once they have had their first major success – not only reaching a long list of corporate objectives, but also achieving an outstanding achievement on a truly business-critical issue. They learn to focus on the areas where they personally need to make a clear and distinct difference, and deliver exceptional quality on these specific areas while effectively managing and delegating other tasks within the organization.

At the same time, as a condition for the transition to the next stage, they need to learn how to manage their energy well and develop good habits to stay fresh, agile and carefree even under massive pressure. Through this transformation, they are becoming cool and relaxed about the normal day-to-day craziness and responsibilities they face, and they organize their life ruthlessly so that they can make a unique and decisive difference as leaders, while responsibly delegating and having their teams and organization take care of the rest.

From ready for success to playful

In the last stage of their development to sustainable top performance, executives make the transformation from being ready for success to actually achieving sustained success and, finally, becoming playful in their role.

At this stage, executives are the masters of their chosen area of expertise, and have strong people and teams around them. They set extremely high standards for themselves; they know what they need to do to achieve true enterprise success. They have learned to handle the pressures that come with their roles with a laser-focus on the one hand, and a healthy degree of coolness and relaxation on the other. They perform with sustained excellence at this highest level by being comfortable in their own skin. To the people around them, they project that they have things under control and enjoy their work and life. You invariably find them in a good mood and laughing almost on a daily basis. They have maximized their Melting Point.

Ultimately, as Apple's legendary boss Steve Jobs once observed, they can even afford to sometimes "Be childish, be foolish". What he meant by this was to be as enthusiastic and experimental as in the first stage ("drawn in"), prepared to break with convention, "think the unthinkable" and risk failure in order to achieve breakthrough innovation. Of course, this stage also involves leaders being very much responsible for, and caring for, the individuals in their teams and ensuring collective organizational success. And enjoying it!

PROGRESSING THROUGH STAGES

These psychological performance stages are not at all rigid, but involve fluid transitions. Throughout a career, executives may make numerous career moves. With every career move or promotion, they start back at the early phases of the model. Let's create a broad example of a young manager. When he or she joins the company, after a period of being very drawn in to their work, then obsessed, they will eventually master their first management role – ultimately becoming playful. Their strong performance will be recognized, and then follows a promotion to a middle management position. In most cases, the new role is attractive to them because it provides new and interesting challenges and is most often a step up. In this more challenging environment, their development initially reverts to the earlier stages – fundamentally drawn in to the new role. But since there is often little time to get on the top of the role, there is a steep learning curve that is most often only possible with a lot of additional effort, which is the phase of being obsessed. There is still the aspiration to mastery and playfulness, although it may be increasingly difficult to achieve.

The big challenge is then to identify when and where an executive can make a unique and distinct significant difference. This means that they need to first focus on delivering their best and most focused efforts, while at the same time being ruthlessly organized, delegating and letting go of certain tasks that the organization can handle independently.

With each career step, the cycle repeats. Having successfully mastered the performance transformation in previous roles, it will be easier (and faster) to progress through those stages when being promoted to an even higher level, if not the highest level, of the organization. This is the stage where top performance becomes sustainable and enjoyable.

AVOID STALLING

At any stage, some top corporate performers are happy to have found something they really enjoy, and are content to stay where they are from a career perspective, perhaps leaving themselves space to build up other aspects of their lives in parallel.

For many corporate performers, however, when they connect their ambition with their attraction to, and passion for, their work, there is a high probability that they want to step up the career ladder.

Depending on how systematically an organization develops their talents, and what opportunities are available, the time it takes to move up the career ladder can vary, from quite slow to very fast. In either case, there is always a danger of career stall.

The image of an airplane stalling mid-flight is helpful in illustrating how a high-flying career can falter.

An airplane stall can best be described as the situation where there is not enough air flowing over the upper side of the wings to create the amount of lift needed to hold up the plane. It is potentially catastrophic, bringing the plane down if not rapidly rectified by the sophisticated intervention of the pilot who needs to gain speed in order to negate the dangerous situation.

A corporate performer may similarly stall when they aspire to climb too fast with insufficient energy and coolness to overcome daily challenges, moments of change, and additional pressure.

Typically, executives love what they do, but they start to feel some additional pain points that come with their all-consuming commitment to it. They might find it hard to disconnect from work, feel frequently tired, may have trouble sleeping, and suffer from impaired or dysfunctional relationships at work and at home.

Life for these corporate performers then becomes very stressful. It can easily lead to a further downward spiral and, inevitably, they run the risk of stalling.

This is particularly dangerous during the stages of a career where the biggest ascent takes place (in the stages **obsessed**, and **ready for success**). There is not much space to get out of a potential stall in these stages. It's like when the aircraft is departing from the runway climbing too fast, any kind of stall will be particularly dangerous because of the lack of opportunity to descend.

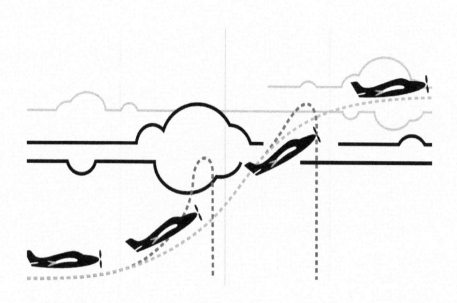

Maintaining controlled, forward momentum and avoiding career stall

Once you realize the early warnings signs of potential stalling, the immediate course correction is crucial in order to survive without damage. In this situation, one wrong decision can lead to full stalling, and may also result in an accelerated downwards spin which is called the spiral stall – it is almost uncontrollable and therefore the most lethal.

In such a case, an individual doesn't really lose their underlying passion – just as the airplane still has powerful engines to give it forward thrust – but they temporarily lose their motivation and enthusiasm to perform at a sustainably high level due to the perceived massive resistance. They get stuck. They are also likely to lose their focus on the crucial issues of importance and become prone to making poor decisions. As a consequence, they are no longer able to inspire their teams and achieve exceptional results. Their performance is often adequate, but not outstanding. They deliver unexceptional performance at a very high price.

With an aircraft, various factors, including the weight of the plane, flaps, and ice, can change the angle of flight at which it stalls. Remember, stalling uses massive energy and leads to a high usage of fuel and is therefore not sustainable. Similarly, executives with overheated engines can quickly stall, taking an increasingly heavy toll on their health and happiness – and leading to a further fall in their performance.

Aircraft stalls are unforgiving and must be rectified promptly to avoid disaster due to rapid altitude loss; an airplane can only stall a certain number of times until it reaches the ground and crashes.

The very same can be said of executives, who cannot risk the damaging effects of constantly having to address crises. Executives must decisively address specific elements that raise the inevitable heat, in order to sustain their top performance and to avoid their careers crashing. How? By gaining the necessary awareness and raising their Performance Melting Point.

CHAPTER 4

UNDERSTANDING YOUR MELTING POINT

I was once introduced to a senior executive in a large global organization. He said, "You know, for many years we have selected our internal talents based on the criterion 'Can they stand the heat?'. Our board's attitude was, 'If you can't stand the heat, get out of the kitchen'. But over the years, I have realized that this approach has meant we haven't made best use of the potential of our internal talents – can you help our top talents to withstand the heat?"

A key success factor for business leaders, executives and corporate performers to sustainably deliver world-class performance is the ability to raise their Melting Point.

Our Melting Point is the critical psychological threshold that all of us face when put under massive stress and pressure. It is the point at which we can no longer control our thinking, emotions and behaviors in an impactful way. It is the moment where we start to internally derail, show dysfunctional behaviors, perform below our best and make mistakes. It is the point where individuals might even abandon their situation without winning and walk away, because the pressure is simply too much to bear. Despite all their passion for what they do, the circumstances are too "hot" for them. They feel they can no longer meet the challenges and demands of their role. They experience a sort of panic.

So what creates a person's Melting Point and how can they adjust it? To what extent is it natural or genetic and how much is it learned as a consequence of their environment or conditioning?

To me, there are three factors that interact to determine an individual's Melting Point:

1. **The psychological constitution: mental and emotional robustness**

2. **The perception and interpretation of the situational pressures from the inner and outer worlds**

3. **The perception and interpretation of the constant pressures from the outer worlds**

FACTOR 1: PSYCHOLOGICAL CONSTITUTION

I believe we all have our own basic mental and emotional constitution, which determines how much we can take before we melt down. Fundamentally, as a performer, it is crucial to build up one's robustness to the degree where "heat" does not hinder our ability to perform at the maximum level.

There is an optimal level of mental and emotional robustness that allows sustainable top performance. It is the state when we are mentally and emotionally robust enough to show our best side, our full potential. We are in sync and connected with our purpose, and our mental, emotional, and physical sides so that we are best able to care for the business, the people around us and ourselves.

There is an important interplay between the psychological constitution of an individual and how much mental and emotional strength they will need to build up. Put simply, the less mental and emotional robustness there is in the psychological constitution, the more systematic build-up is necessary.

I see two areas that are potentially dangerous when considering an individual's basic constitution: too little and too much mental and emotional robustness. Performers who have too little robustness easily become victims and won't be able to take enough responsibility for their actions and the results. Performers who have too much robustness may become over-assertive, even bullying, and are not capable of building the necessary long-term, empathy-based relationships for sustainable success despite their achievements.

So where do you stand? How would you characterize yourself?

FACTOR 2: SITUATIONAL PRESSURES FROM THE INNER AND OUTER WORLDS

How do individuals perceive and interpret their current *situational* pressures? How much stress and anxiety has been created in the last couple of days, weeks and recent months as a result of these pressures? For example, if you have become the latest member of an executive team, you are faced with the new pressure of being part of the highest level of an organization. This is a situation that has not been experienced before. Then, the organization may go through a significant restructuring that is a first of its kind. So, on top of the new pressure of being a member of the executive team, you have to co-lead the restructuring process. And maybe, at the same time, you have to move your family over to the company's new location. When your situation suddenly changes in a lot of different ways, and you enter new, uncharted territory, how do you react? Do you feel sudden anxiety and crippling self-doubt? Or do you feel in control, focused and ready to take on the challenge?

FACTOR 3: CONSTANT PRESSURES FROM THE OUTER WORLDS

Then there are the *constant* pressures that come with the position that you have, the everyday stresses and complexities that characterize the role. To stay with the example mentioned earlier, as a member of an executive team you are simply expected to perform a broad variety of highly impactful tasks, such as presenting to the board or in front of large audiences; short-term traveling into different time-zones; designing and managing an effective organization and developing a vision for its future success; and having difficult conversations and managing conflict. These tasks are considered "normal" for the role, but nevertheless, they are intense and challenging and will take time to master. Are these aspects of the role creating a lot of stress for you? Or do you feel energized and inspired?

HOW ARE THESE THREE FACTORS INTERRELATED?

There is an important interplay between an individual's basic psychological constitution and the way that they perceive the pressures in their environment. Let's take an example of an executive whose psychological constitution is defined by a natural or learned strong ability to withstand pressure. If the other two factors are low – that they perceive little negative situational pressures as well as little negative constant pressures – then the given situation will not even get close to the individual's Melting Point. The perceived pressures and challenges are not enough that the individual would experience a high amount of stress.

However, it is much more likely that when the perceived situational pressures and the constant pressures from the outer world are very high, then top business performers depend on a strong mental and emotional robustness.

Here is an example of a top performer who is facing a unique set of pressures – situational and constant – related to a new career development. The combination of factors led to him reaching his Melting Point:

IN THEIR OWN WORDS: REACHING THE MELTING POINT

A few years ago I was very close to a meltdown. I got offered one of the top jobs in my organization, with lots of responsibility and opportunities to prove that I could significantly impact the results of the company. Always in my career, I had been a guy who was positive and optimistic about what I could bring to the table, and confident that I would be successful in new roles pretty fast. This time, however, my internal perception started to change quite soon.

It's easy to trace the original starting point for my problems, which was when my wife and I got divorced. Of course, this caused a massive personal crisis at the time, especially because we have three young children. Although I have always been quite mentally tough, this period was hard on all of us. For a long time, I felt like I was able to cope with it, although it was a very difficult road.

With the support of family and friends at home, and colleagues at work, I was able to get back on my feet very quickly and everything seemed fairly normal, at least on the surface. I managed to perform reasonably well at work. But all the time there were problems and pressures building up within me as a result of the big changes that I had been going through recently.

The truth was that in my new situation, I felt increasingly trapped, like a hamster running in its wheel – trying to do everything well at work and at home and feeling exhausted all the time.

From the outside, I gave the impression that I was doing well. But the fatigue of this "new normal" was taking its toll. I began to realize that I could not go on like this, feeling exhausted both physically and mentally.

My promotion was a very mixed blessing. As far as the outside world was concerned, it was great: it proved I had the confidence of my boss, the CEO of our company; that I was a capable guy and that I was ready to move to the next level in the organization, taking on major new responsibilities. But the truth was that I never had to lead such a large group of people. That was a much bigger challenge than anything I'd been used to and I was under constant pressure to prove that I could do it. I was in a very, very stressful situation, because at the time we were under massive budget restrictions.

Under these circumstances, I was very unsure if I could win the respect of my team or of my fellow managers at this new level. I found it very hard to adapt. Deep inside, I was lacking self-confidence and had a lot of doubts: "Will my team truly accept me? Will I be tough enough to make the changes that must be made? Will I be able to lead my organization effectively?"

Matters were made even worse because I was having problems with some of my key relationships at work. In particular, I was trapped in a pretty tense situation between myself and my boss, the CEO of the company, who was always on my back asking for a progress update on a daily basis.

I had flexibility over my office hours, and I always took work home with me – this badly affected my family life. I was not really engaged with my children when we were together. I felt a massive guilt about this, probably even more so than many other working parents, because my children had just been through a difficult transition with the divorce. I felt that they deserved better.

Even though I thought I could shoulder a lot, the aftermath of the incredibly stressful job, the current additional situational components combined with the divorce became almost too much to bear. I used to be a confident leader who thought he could do almost anything – and for the first time in my career I felt real anxiety, doubts and fear of making wrong decisions.

I had clearly reached my Melting Point.

CHAPTER 5

WHAT CREATES THE HEAT FOR YOU?

There are many different elements that can increase the "heat" and have a significant negative impact, causing previously high-achieving corporate champions to no longer perform to the best of their ability. In some cases, one specific element can be so strong and inflamed that it can cause an executive to reach their Melting Point, stalling their career and adversely affecting their health and domestic happiness. You can think of these elements as "pain points", that when combined with other situational factors can lead to meltdown.

If an individual opts to "live with the pain", staying in post and taking little or no remedial action, these elements are likely to have an ongoing negative impact on their ability to be constantly at their personal best. The pain points will also undermine their professional effectiveness, with knock-on effects on their teams and their organizations that will naturally feel the adverse effects of the executive's impaired leadership. Sustained periods of ineffectiveness lead to career stagnation or even stall.

The following section will help you identify the specific elements that can raise the heat for you, potentially leading you to the point of melting. Many elements listed on the following pages might be familiar to you, some may be new; they have been raised most often in the many interviews conducted with senior leaders and executives as research for this book. It is not an exhaustive list – it is important that you evaluate your unique situation and identify which elements increase the heat for you personally.

Please take good note that the elements do not create the same heat for everybody. Understanding the elements most present for you will help you gain clarity and the ability to prioritize the areas that must be addressed with urgency.

ELEMENTS THAT CAN RAISE THE HEAT:

1. Modern business complexity and ambiguity

2. A long-hours culture and overwork

3. Office politics

4. Travel torment

5. Executive isolation

6. Wanting to do everything and difficulty in delegating

7. Dysfunctional personality traits

8. Letting work take over at home

9. Fatigue

10. Always "on"

11. Career moves

12. Redundancy

13. Domestic changes

14. Family crisis

15. Health issues

ELEMENT 1: MODERN BUSINESS COMPLEXITY AND AMBIGUITY

Alongside work overload has come increased business complexity, born of globalization and the communications revolution. Executives in multinational companies have been, and remain, in the frontline of these changes. Frequently, they occupy more than one specific role in their organization – they become leaders of multiple roles and projects. This often adds a lot of ambiguity to their situation.

ELEMENT 2: A LONG-HOURS CULTURE AND OVERWORK

Overwork is one of the most common pain points for ambitious businesspeople. Ambitious corporate performers invariably find themselves facing a daunting workload that is exacerbated by their own success: the more milestones they achieve, the more key tasks and multiple roles they are given, especially in times when budgets are being cut. With too much work to do, and increasingly "elastic" timeframes in which they are expected to do it, executives extend their working day, starting early in the morning and working late into the evening. Today's corporate culture is very often about long hours and the expectation that leaders should be available all day, every day.

ELEMENT 3: OFFICE POLITICS

As if the external environment does not present enough challenges, another common potential source of stress in today's corporate culture is the issue of office politics; with relationships between overstretched executives, their bosses, peers and direct reports often showing signs of strain. Difficult relationships, people driving their own agendas, and dysfunctional team dynamics for personal advantage, can be extremely difficult for some individuals to navigate, especially during times of organizational change.

ELEMENT 4: TRAVEL TORMENT

For many business leaders, relentless international travel is another stressful symptom of today's complex, globalized business environment. It takes a physical and mental toll that includes jetlag as well as exposure to different climate-zones and health-related factors that cannot always be controlled. It might start with simple examples such as the neighboring passenger on a long-haul flight who sneezes the whole time, exposing you to their cold or flu.

ELEMENT 5: EXECUTIVE ISOLATION

As one approaches the top echelons of an organization, it can be a lonely environment, often lacking the camaraderie found at lower levels in the hierarchy. Feelings of isolation will be compounded by awkward peer-to-peer relationships, and when executives are unable to share the burden of the challenges they face, it may potentially be difficult to deal effectively with the causes of anxiety and stress.

ELEMENT 6: WANTING TO DO EVERYTHING AND DIFFICULTY IN DELEGATING

Perhaps because of feeling isolated – and sometimes also because it is in their own perfectionist nature – some executives feel pressured by their environment to micromanage, striving to achieve too many objectives personally. They lack the ability to focus on the areas where they personally must make a clear and distinct difference, and take almost everything on their shoulders. Even when they command significant resources and lead numerous direct reports and teams, they struggle to trust others, delegate tasks effectively and let go to personally focus on the things that matter the most.

ELEMENT 7: DYSFUNCTIONAL PERSONALITY TRAITS

Executives can make their situation worse through their own dysfunctional personality traits: the desire for perfection; being distrustful to others when under pressure; the excessive need to please others (especially top management or the Board); or a tendency to be melodramatic during times of conflict. These unhelpful traits become overexpressed in very stressful situations and can have a very negative impact on effective leadership and team engagement. It is important to carefully manage those responses. When dysfunctional behavior (even unconscious) goes unaddressed, there is a high likelihood that a leader's team will eventually stop supporting them ("he is a nice guy unless he is under stress").

ELEMENT 8: LETTING WORK TAKE OVER AT HOME

In such an intense environment, the majority of executives are taking work home with them, not just occasionally but habitually, which can cause a ripple effect on their family lives, and serious ramifications for their own health and happiness. When work consistently takes over at home, too little room is left for fulfilling relationships and leisure.

ELEMENT 9: FATIGUE

Problems with diet, exercise and sleep are not confined to executives who travel a lot. Long working hours and a sedentary lifestyle, with many hours spent at their desks or in meetings, means that many executives face challenges around eating, exercising and sleeping sufficiently to maintain their energy levels and their basic health, fitness and wellbeing.

ELEMENT 10: ALWAYS "ON"

Alongside the tangible issue of taking work tasks home, many executives complain of the mental and emotional problem of taking their work – and their professional worries – home with them. They find it difficult to switch off from their careers and transition effectively from their work to their domestic and family lives.

ELEMENT 11: CAREER MOVES

The prospect of a new job – either a promotion, or a move to a new company – can be exciting and daunting at the same time. It involves new responsibilities, new relationships, and pressure to demonstrate results as soon as possible. To cope with understandable anxiety, it is important to go back to the basics of your fitness, and at the same time assess the challenges and expectations of the new role and environment in a strategic way, in order to have a good and smooth start.

ELEMENT 12: REDUNDANCY

Many executives will face the prospect of redundancy at some point in their careers and, whether it's anticipated or not, voluntary or forced, it's an issue that needs a careful and considered approach. Understanding your strengths and weighing your professional options should be balanced alongside your personal circumstances, such as your health and family obligations. Any opportunities that arise need to be handled in alignment with your core values and overall vision, so as to make the right decision, rather than simply grasping the first or easiest option.

ELEMENT 13: DOMESTIC CHANGES

Joyous and life-changing events, such as the birth of a child and transitioning to parenthood, can at times have a significant professional impact, such as adding fatigue. It requires time to adapt and regain balance on a new level for all working parents. And at some point in their career, most executives will cope with aging parents who may be facing declining health. Taking the time to spend meaningful moments with parents, and organizing care, are important additional activities that require time and emotional energy.

ELEMENT 14: FAMILY CRISES

An individual's career can easily be derailed by a personal tragedy such as an accident, a loved one's illness, or the death of a family member or close friend. Death, divorce and illness present major challenges and, until we experience them, we can never really know how we will react. It's important for executives to understand the need to treat themselves kindly at such sensitive times. For some, working themselves to a standstill may be a coping mechanism – a form of escape from the problem in their personal life – but ultimately it may serve to delay the healing process. Communication is key, whether that means discussing the implications of what has happened with your family and friends, or letting your organization know why you need some additional flexibility in your work schedule for a period.

ELEMENT 15: HEALTH ISSUES

A number of my clients – some of them in highly influential executive roles – have experienced the situation of a personal health issue. They were diagnosed for example with a chronic disease, cancer or another serious illness. Serious illness can result from a wide variety of factors – environmental factors as well as genetic disposition. What is most critical is finding the peace and transparency to make successful treatment and a healthy rehabilitation the absolute priority. Ideally, this is done in connection with the organization to provide additional support, making it possible for a meaningful return to work after rehabilitation.

CONSEQUENCES OF "LIVING WITH THE PAIN"

Every corporate performer, at one time or another, will suffer from some of these heat-raising elements. They may even pride themselves on how much pain and suffering they can bear. But long-term, coping with ever-present pain can carry a heavy toll. What is the impression you make on your spouse if you come home totally exhausted every evening and all you can do is fall asleep on the sofa? You may be very successful at work, but then when you get home, there is very little of you left. You just crash. Once in a while, this may be an acceptable pattern. But when it becomes a regular occurrence, it is not sustainable. It may lead to personal disaster: to divorces, to poor quality relationships with children and friends, and potentially impaired performance at work.

For some executives, it is not necessarily a specific element that threatens to undermine their professional performance, but a more general sense of dissatisfaction – a pervasive feeling that their personal lives and their high-flying careers are constantly out of harmony with each other. They experience a very real fear that something will give if the situation is left unaddressed and they are not integrated more positively. The long-term consequence can be a persistent lack of joy and peace. This is a very steep price to pay.

When top performers reach their Melting Point, it is never simply the result of situational and constant pressures. It is compounded by the elements mentioned above combined with their basic psychological constitution.

Let me share a story of a client in this situation:

IN THEIR OWN WORDS: IDENTIFYING ELEMENTS THAT RAISE THE HEAT

I was in a situation where I was very successful in my organization. But despite my success, I was suffering.

First, I had more work on my plate than I ever could potentially accomplish. To some extent this was my own fault: I achieved a lot of milestones, and people would pile additional tasks onto me and I did not say 'no' enough.

I suffered from being too much of a pleaser. I had a good boss and I enjoyed working with her, but she was the kind of boss who would not stop asking for as much as possible from me. I should have said, 'Up to here okay, but no further', but I was not able to draw this sort of boundary. This has been a persistent problem for me throughout my career.

In addition, one of my huge stumbling blocks was my desire to have everything under full control all the time, to the point of micromanagement. Rather than seeing the big picture, I would try to get involved in the fine detail of too many projects. Obviously, if you have hundreds of people reporting to you, as I did, this is a clear path to failure – you will not get the job done.

I desperately needed to develop strategies to prioritize, delegate, coach, let go and also to manage in an effective way, upward, outward and downward.

At the same time, my team and I were in a very high-stress environment. There was the feeling that we had to work 24/7. We felt there was an expectation that we had to be available at all times. Given that we worked for a company with headquarters on another continent, because of time zone differences, we had many meetings scheduled for 6am or 7am, or 8pm or 9pm, to accommodate our head office.

Colleagues and clients were able to contact me by phone and email at any time of the day or night. There was also an expectation that everything would be handled promptly – that if there was an urgent email out there, we should have seen it. It didn't matter if it was the weekend. Even on a Sunday afternoon, if I didn't respond to an email, I might receive a phone call from the CEO saying, 'Did you check your emails? There is this issue and we need your response.' His intensity was just immense.

I was aware that I was working extremely hard, but still seemed to struggle to do the right things to be sustainably successful. I realized that I needed to find a different way of keeping my performance at a level where I could fulfil the expectations of my people as well as meet my own high standards.

It wasn't just about the output that the company needed; it was about 'what does my body need, and my mind and my spirit?'. We give so much if we are in high-level positions in corporations and there is this constant risk that there is nothing left for us in the home environment.

I took this kind of dissatisfaction home with me, so I was not a happy person there either. I am somebody who gives everything at work and I would go home tired in the evening and just slump. I would be fully engaged at work, fully attentive, and then when I got home I wouldn't have the same energy.

I found it difficult to differentiate between my work and private life. Because of the demands of the job, I could never fully let go, not even for short periods of time. So I was stressed by this and my husband and family found it frustrating that work was always present in our family life.

My energy level flowing between my private life and my professional life was way out of balance. At some point I could only generate and mobilize energy for work. There was no energy left for any other parts of my life.

Physically, I went into decline. I didn't sleep well and I was stressed out all the time. I had to travel a lot in my role, and the travelling made me constantly tired – and when I was tired I tended to eat too much and not exercise enough.

At only 42 years old, I developed serious back problems and I gained weight. I was not very fat but I was at least five to seven kilos more than I should have been, and that didn't help.

My team was suffering from the same kind of issues that I was. The universal theme was the intensity that the job was putting on everybody's personal life. Everyone was saying that they had never encountered anything like it before.

At my best, I am a very action-oriented person. I am someone who really delivers. But what I was missing was a sense of joy, peace and calmness in my life.

Although I fundamentally loved my work I realized that I needed to find a different way to make my top performance sustainable. The thought of doing my day-to-day job for another couple of years gave me little motivation. I was often thin-skinned and short-tempered. I had to go through a performance transformation to regain my lightness and my cool in order to make the distinctive decisions that would impact the business and my future career in a positive way. Having clearly identified the elements that had raised the heat for me was one of the major achievements and was the foundation for a successful performance transformation."

CHAPTER 6

RAISING YOUR MELTING POINT

You have seen through various examples how an individual can reach their Melting Point, the critical psychological threshold that arises when individuals are faced with enormous intensity and pressure. You can see all too clearly the risk, professional and personal, of melting in the face of pressure: low or mediocre business performance, dissatisfaction at work, poor results and career stall.

As discussed in Chapter 4, the Melting Point can be highly individual, and is determined by three specific factors: an individual's psychological constitution; their perceived situational challenges; and the constant pressures that they experience. In Chapter 3, we discussed the Executive Performance Transformation: the four psychological stages an individual can move through in their career, from drawn in, to obsessed, to ready for success, and even playful. However, many potential heat-raising elements can interfere with this transformation, as seen in Chapter 5, and lead an individual to reach their Melting Point. When this happens, the consequences can be potentially catastrophic.

Business leaders, executives, ambitious managers and corporate performers need to increase their coolness and resilience to the intense heat of their position and the pressures of today's scorching business environment.

So how can an individual remain cool in difficult conditions and raise their Melting Point? And what does it take to achieve the ultimate level of performance: approaching their work in an energized and playful way?

The core foundation of success and sustainable high performance is found in the following concept: **Personal Leadership Excellence.**

WHAT IS PERSONAL LEADERSHIP EXCELLENCE?

Highly successful executives reveal strong parallels in how they perform at their personal best and build a successful career. The key characteristics are the six P's of Personal Leadership Excellence:

Passion, Precision, Perception, Peace, Presence and Persistence.

Personal Leadership Excellence stems from executives harmonizing their "inner world" of mental, emotional and physical health and their "outer world", which is dominated by the demands of their leadership roles and other relevant, even private demands.

Our P6PROP® model of Personal Leadership Excellence is an established – and sophisticated – business instrument that helps business leaders, executives, top corporate performers and ambitious managers achieve and maintain optimal performance, especially during times of uncertainty and change. The concept and the mechanics behind the six P-components are the core foundation of success and sustainable high performance.

Personal Leadership Excellence fundamentally enables executives to make the performance transformation from overburdened, highly-stressed victims of today's frenetic business world, into business champions who don't merely survive, but flourish in this environment in a playful way, finding purpose, success and fulfilment in it. To do so, they must find the all-important harmonization between their inner and outer worlds, creating alignment in their own professional and personal lives.

Additionally, they need to specifically apply specific behavioral patterns to raise their Melting Point.

HOW TO RAISE YOUR MELTING POINT

There are **ten key behavioral patterns** that will give you the concrete guidance to stay cool under pressure and deliver sustained world-class business performance under massive intensity.

From the following list, you must identify which of the behavioral patterns you need to consistently apply on a daily basis, based on your diagnostics of your psychological constitution and the specific heat-creating elements you are confronted with.

TEN KEY BEHAVIORAL PATTERNS TO RAISE YOUR MELTING POINT

- Defining and connecting with your deeper purpose

- Preparing for your key performance moments

- Making progress

- Adopting good habits to save 30 percent of your energy beyond work

- Establishing boundaries

- Performing with reserves

- Managing office politics

- Creating and cultivating a network of inspirational people

- Mentally transitioning between work and home

- Disconnecting

DEFINING AND CONNECTING WITH YOUR DEEPER PURPOSE:

One key behavioral pattern of Personal Leadership Excellence is that you clearly understand your story so far, from a professional and personal point of view. Based on that, you need to identify the functional parts of your story that you would like to continue and build upon, and also the dysfunctional parts that you would like to replace – especially the thought patterns and behaviors that hold you back from staying cool. Understanding your core values and your fundamental purpose (personal and professional) is the basis for creating an inspiring vision that you can use as your guiding star in important fundamental decisions, such as why you would like to pursue a career as an executive in such a challenging environment. I recommend that you write all this down and regularly read through your fundamental purpose and your core values – especially in times of huge pressure and intensity.

To raise your Melting Point:

Start each day by taking 5 minutes in the early morning before you start work to read your core values, your deeper purpose and your vision.

PREPARING FOR YOUR KEY PERFORMANCE MOMENTS:

In order to make a clear and specific difference for your organization, you need to identify the key performance areas where you personally have to be at your best. This could be running an important presentation, speaking publicly, or developing a concept with major strategic impact. These are the moments where you need to shine. This means, of course, top quality preparation. Equally, you must prepare yourself mentally and emotionally to be at your personal best as you deliver on these key performance moments: for example, presenting with a certain (and adequate) lightness; and engaging the audience and absorbing potential critical voices with seriousness and charm.

To raise your Melting Point:

Develop a ritual at the beginning of every new month, where you carefully look into all the activities that your organization and your teams need to perform. Then, clearly identify YOUR key performance moments and make it a priority to prepare as much as possible. On the specific day when you will execute the performance, connect yourself mentally and emotionally with your core values and your characteristics as a performer that will ensure you are at your best and most robust.

MAKING PROGRESS:

The key to sustaining high motivation is to feel you are making progress on a daily basis. In an environment where you could work 24/7 and still never be done, it is crucial that you maintain your day-to-day motivation. It is very frustrating to "work" for 10-12 hours and leave the office feeling like you haven't made any progress on what really needs your attention. Instead, you sat all day in meetings or dealt with issues that had little strategic impact. After such a day, it is easy to feel like it was not a good day at work, or the day was wasted.

It is therefore absolutely crucial that you set priorities on a daily basis so that you can make progress on the relevant tasks that need your personal focus and with that, allow yourself to have a good day at work.

To raise your Melting Point:

Schedule two 40-minute blocks of time every day – your "focus cycle". During this focus time, you only work on a key task without interruption, allowing you to make significant progress. You will then experience the feeling that your time was well spent, and it was a good day at work – because you actually made progress.

ADOPTING GOOD HABITS TO SAVE 30 PERCENT OF YOUR ENERGY BEYOND WORK:

Good habits create positive reinforcements in your life. Making conscious decisions to eliminate damaging habits that have become very deeply ingrained, and replacing them with good habits that offer a multitude of benefits, can have a major positive impact. Learning helpful routines and rituals make the good habits stick. Although you may think you don't have the time to build up new behaviors, these good habits will actually help you save time in the long run, as you become a more efficient and productive self.

Focus on your diet, exercise and sleep. Consider reducing the size of the portion on your plate, introducing healthy snacks between meals, eating light, and drinking fewer alcoholic and caffeinated drinks. Following a sports and exercise routine with 2-3 sessions of resistance training and 2-3 of aerobic training per week is important to get rid of the stress reactions in your body. Taking regular breaks during the work days where you briefly disconnect and get some movement is vital. All these measures, and more, can significantly help your performance by day and your sleep patterns at night. Careful management of diet, exercise, breaks and sleep can also help to counter travel fatigue. Remember, almost all top performers know exactly how to recover. Recognizing when you are running out of energy and being able to identify ways in which you can rest, recuperate and re-energize is decisive.

Restoring balance and vigor to your body can have a range of positive impacts on your life. So many of us know deep down what habits we should be adopting, but until we actually make these lifestyle changes, we can't reap the rewards.

> **To raise your Melting Point:**
> Strategically manage your energy during each business day so that you leave the office with 30 percent of your energy left. This will allow you to perform your last task at work with focus and intensity, and also to truly connect at home and have fulfilling moments outside work. This means for example not going home completely exhausted.

ESTABLISHING BOUNDARIES:

Stay focused and aware of the importance of your domestic life as well as your professional obligations. This requires good interpersonal communication and practicing assertiveness, an important skill that can be learned. It means being clear about what you can deliver, to stand up for yourself and courteously explain to bosses or colleagues why certain requests or expectations may be unrealistic or unreasonable, or that tasks need to be prioritized. This will make you a trustworthy, transparent and honest team member.

Make a substantial effort to inform your family of upcoming business commitments. Tell them if you're going to be delayed by work. If you see a heavy schedule on the horizon that will involve you being away from home a great deal, warn them in advance and agree to make it up to them afterwards. Making a commitment like this to your family (and honoring it) is just as important as setting limits at work.

> **To raise your Melting Point:**
> Plan deliberate actions with your most significant people and relationships, especially in times of massive intensity. At work, ensure constant communication and alignment with your manager, peers and teams through ritualized meetings. At home, agree to spend (at least) 90 minutes together, where you leave mobile devices behind, to help keep the focus on each other.

PERFORMING WITH RESERVES:

Organize yourself in such a way that you can generally operate and deliver your top performance at 90 to 95 percent of your energy levels. At your highest level of performance, you will very often be confronted with unplanned, extraordinary tasks that you will need to complete. Be ready for that. If you are habitually operating at 100 percent, you will always need to invest unplanned extra effort for these additional tasks. Therefore, you will always have the feeling that work has taken over – and you will risk not being able to develop the necessary energy and focus to deliver on the key "must-win" tasks.

To raise your Melting Point:

At the beginning of every year, month, and week, determine the areas where you personally need to make substantial progress and where the organization needs your involvement and focus. Make a plan to achieve this substantial progress with 90 to 95 percent of your energy levels (not time), while properly delegating the other tasks within the rest of the organization.

MANAGING OFFICE POLITICS:

How many times have we heard people say, "It's not the job that gets me down, it's the office politics"? This doesn't have to be the case, but to change things we have to learn to deal with problem situations and strained relationships, and develop techniques to defuse them. You can do this firstly by replacing the word "politics" with "relationships". You will achieve a much more positive attitude to this topic, which is essential to success in a corporate environment.

> **To raise your Melting Point:**
> Map out your political (relationship!) environment and identify the key relationships before interacting to your stakeholder network. After having mapped out your environment, start healthy networking activities with important people in your professional network on a weekly basis.

CREATING AND CULTIVATING A NETWORK OF INSPIRATIONAL PEOPLE:

As an executive or business leader, you are investing a lot of time in delivering and ensuring top performance. When you reach a certain level in your organization, it is difficult to find time and spontaneous opportunities to meet up with inspiring people who can provide you with insights and new perspectives. For your own inspiration and development, I therefore recommend that you build up and cultivate a network of people who will encourage you, challenge you, support you, help you reflect and think differently about the problems and challenges that you face daily. This network can include experts in your field, mentors, or coaches. In your private life, make strong and inspiring relationships with your family and friends a top priority.

> **To raise your Melting Point:**
> Keep a list of those that inspire you most and as a ritual take it out every second week to plan one or two actions: going for lunch, scheduling calls, keeping in touch. Take deliberate time out to personally meet the people outside of the workplace to get new perspectives.

MENTALLY TRANSITIONING BETWEEN WORK AND HOME:

The transition from work to home – and back again – is vitally important, so you do not just turn up mentally and emotionally ill-prepared for your new environment. If you have had a busy day, and your head is full, think about how you want to be when you go home. Use the journey to work, and returning home, to make the transition, so you do not just walk in the door and find yourself suddenly thrown into situations that you are not ready to face. Establishing rituals that will detach you from work and connect you with home in the evening (and vice-versa in the morning) is critical. You can do this by "Checking in" with your best side before entering the work place.

A big part of making a successful transition from the world of work to the domestic environment is regaining control over "always-on" technology, which so easily intrudes into our personal and family lives. Developing a ritual for tuning out technology may take time to get used to, but it really does help you focus on the here and now.

> **To raise your Melting Point:**
>
> Take a few minutes of silence to get mentally and emotionally ready to be at your personal best at work by visualizing yourself perfectly connected with your core values. Do this every day before you enter the workplace, and especially when you have an important performance to deliver. Do the same "check in" with your best side as you transition from work to home. Visualize yourself at your personal best in the private environment before connecting with the people at home.

DISCONNECTING:

Rituals at the end of the day help you achieve inner calm, a clear head and, most importantly, the right frame of mind in which to experience deep and rejuvenating sleep. I strongly recommend disconnecting from work on a daily basis for 90 minutes, ideally, when you come home in the evening. Putting all devices away in one specific room at home, like your dedicated office or computer room, is key. Make this one of your most important principles. Only make an exception if there is a true business emergency.

To raise your Melting Point:

Protect your private space in your home, defining only one room where you allow work to take place. In particular, no devices should be taken into the bedroom, which needs to be associated only with rest and recovery.

I have been asked the following question many times: when is it the perfect time to develop Personal Leadership Excellence and learn how to raise the Melting Point? Well, there is no clear specific time to do so – you can do this potentially at any stage in your career.

For those who are still relatively early in their career, organizations usually provide the time to develop; and some negative or dysfunctional patterns may not have become too ingrained and are easier to change. But some leaders realize they are lacking something later in their career, often only after having experienced the inevitable heat. Sometimes they may have even suffered setbacks because of the heat of the situation in which they have to perform. Typically, they are already at a senior level and operating under pressure and scrutiny. In this high pressure environment, they have much less freedom and time to try many different things to develop. As a consequence, the rising temperature felt by an executive might be left unaddressed, and if it gets too much to bear, they will most likely melt. In other words, they might provide poor leadership, maybe even suffer a breakdown and stall in some significant way. Therefore, addressing the pain points in a constructive way, in order to achieve a smooth Executive Performance

Transformation, is crucial for sustained world-class business performance.

Let me continue to share the powerful story of a client who has achieved Performance Leadership Excellence and impressively raised the Melting Point:

RAISING THE MELTING POINT

I realized that, to avoid meltdown and to make my top performance really sustainable, I needed to find a winning mindset. The starting point for me was to chart my own story so far. This showed me what had brought me to where I am, what my core values are and helped me to understand more clearly what is truly important to me. The process helped me come to terms with my vulnerabilities by opening up and being honest with myself and with others.

I had quite a challenging background, and as I really looked deeper at my history, I realized the impact this had on me. I did always feel I was incredibly tough on myself, even sometimes brutal. We were moving houses a lot when I was a child. I never really built up strong relationships – I was afraid that the pain would be too much when we had to move again, so that was one way that I coped.

I realized that I was often disconnected externally and this is still the way I operate. It takes a long time for me to become close to others. I became more aware that for all of my independence, I lacked some deep connections.

I wanted to change this, so I worked at being more at peace with networking activities, such as going for lunch with peers, building a rapport – all things that I had avoided in the past. I made conscious efforts to build a strong team around me. The experience was amazing. I started to ask for help – previously I would always want to achieve everything myself – and got so much more in return from my team than I could ever anticipate. Their support has been a multiplier to my personal and our collective performance!

I learned to understand my unique and distinctive value to our organization. Since then, I have been focusing on making a true difference to the success of the business, much more than delivering a long list of achievements. My organization is able to deliver with the appropriate level of transparency, delegation and empowerment from my side.

In parallel, I have built up my good habits and rituals to make my top performance sustainable.

For example, I started to eat differently to sustain my energy. The content didn't change too much, but the timing did. I used to skip breakfast and eat almost nothing during the day and then a really big meal in the evening. This meant my calorie intake was entirely unbalanced with my need for energy. For a couple of important hours in my work day, I realized that I was hypoglycemic. Now, I'm eating smaller meals throughout the day. I'm not craving food, so I make better choices. To sustain my energy through the day, I snack on the right things: calcium and protein, so for me that means nuts, natural yoghurt and also soy milkshakes. These are things that I always have at my desk now. I have a small snack around every three hours.

I used to drink wine almost every day, not heavily, but to relax in the evening, and I stopped this completely. I only drink alcohol now at the weekend or for special occasions during the week. I also drink a lot more water and herbal tea – at least two liters a day. I can now concentrate for a really long time – sometimes 10 hours of back-to-back meetings, although I'm not sure if that's a good thing!

By limiting how much caffeine I consume, I sleep much better. I wake up more refreshed and can see that it has become easier for me to maintain a relatively stable weight.

I started sports again. I get up very early in the morning and every second day I go for an hour-long run. I had not exercised in years but I made a commitment to do so four days a week. I altered my schedule to get up at 5am, so that I can exercise. I used to stay up late and have a hard time getting out of bed that early in the morning, but I have shifted my whole internal clock and my routine. That was a major change.

I discovered through exercises and medical testing that, although I was good with cardio exercise, I was completely neglecting stretching activities. Now my exercise plan includes yoga for flexibility and also some resistance training for strength.

At first, I was afraid my work performance would suffer if, for example, I went to the gym for an hour during the day to get some proper exercise. But in fact it was the other way around – by giving myself that hour, my performance actually improved. I feel that I am much more energized, focused and engaged in my interactions.

I also keep up my fitness while I am on the road. I have a set of exercises that I can do in a hotel room or at home when I'm not able to go to a fitness center. I would say my personal health is pretty good. I've lost some weight, and my body shape has changed – it's more toned, with more muscle mass and greater flexibility.

My confidence has gone up too. I'm stronger and I stand taller. It just makes such a difference when you feel better about yourself. It changes your whole outlook on life. It makes you so much more positive.

I'm very, very conscious of the importance of family as well as work.

I made a very clear cut-off point when I would stop working in the evening. I used to work until 9pm or 10pm, but now I always stop work so that I can be home at 7pm when I am not traveling, with very rare exceptions. This allows me to spend time with my children before they go to bed.

An important part of this is about separating technology from my home. I keep my work laptop in one location and don't take it with me around the house.

I normally do one last email check at around 9.30pm-10pm, and then I put my laptop in a bag and the bag in a room, and I close the door. I always used to take my *mobile phone to bed; I don't do that anymore. In the hour before bed I am off email and I follow a little ritual to wind down.*

Something I found really helpful was learning a work-to-home transition ritual, and also a home-to-work ritual. Now, when I park up in my driveway every day, arriving home from work, I focus on changing from businessperson to parent. I have to do it consciously every day, but it's very simple. I ask myself, 'How am I feeling? Who do I want to be? What kind of wife and mother do I want to be?' I stop and have that moment of reflection. It takes about three minutes. So I say to myself, 'Okay, I'm transitioning, so what do I need to do differently?' And then it's easy. It's just a mental contemplation until you get into the right zone. That's how I switch from "work mode" to "home mode".

I do the same type of rituals when I arrive at work. By the time I've parked, I've mentally attuned myself for work.

I include my family more in my thinking – what their expectation is of me and what my expectation is of them. We sat down and had some serious talks to clarify our roles and expectations, which I hadn't consciously done before. That really enhanced family life by introducing some new routines – so we always had our Sunday night dinner together, for example – and we had family meetings to talk about what we all wanted to do, how we can help each other, and what our concerns are, so we could understand each other in a clear and more constructive way.

Now, I feel very positive and energetic, so I feel almost as if it doesn't matter what challenges come my way; I always feed on the positive. I feel in control, and I get a lot of creative ideas on how we can improve things. In fact, on average, I get one idea per week. Sharing it with my team on a weekly basis may be too much for them, so I carry a little book with me where I write down all the ideas I have. Once a month, I sit with my direct leadership team and share my ideas. Together, we then decide which ideas will bring us further on a short-, mid- and long-term basis. In those meetings, we encourage everyone to think unconventionally, to be really creative and even "crazy" with their thinking. As you can imagine, we also laugh a lot. It has become a truly enjoyable journey.

Now, I love what I'm doing, I'm proud of what I've achieved and I have the patience and confidence that I can *bring a lot of value. I know what I'm passionate about and I have a clear idea of how I can make progress and where I can make a unique and distinctive difference. I have enough energy to deliver my sustainable top performance and to engage with my family and friends outside work. This clarity is incredibly helpful.*

CONCLUSION

By achieving Personal Leadership Excellence in your professional life and staying cool under pressure – as a business leader, executive, top corporate performer or ambitious manager – you will gain true satisfaction in your career, and constantly perform at your best in a playful way to sustain world-class business performance.

But beyond the obvious personal benefits, how far will this affect your ability to become a genuinely outstanding executive, one who has developed a true enterprise view? How will it help you create collective success, something far more valuable than just individual achievement?

Not only will you fulfil your own performance potential, but through your positive influence on their teams – by spreading the benefits widely throughout your organization – you can also make a huge positive impact on the wider business performance and the bottom line.

Through your leadership, this approach cascades to the teams, who feel comfortable using the same framework and ultimately going through a similar positive performance transformation. While it is one thing for an executive to be appreciated for the content, structure and network, being recognized as an inspiring leader is even more powerful, as it will secure much greater engagement and commitment from everyone in the organization. This will result in a widely-felt positive culture with outcomes for the business as a whole, because the leaders and key performers of your organization will stay cool under massive pressure and mobilize optimal energy levels to deliver on the must-wins.

By having achieved playfulness in your performance, however, you will not only deliver performance on the must-wins, but also constantly renew and adapt your organization to a changing environment. One of the major challenges for organizations is to create new and innovative approaches while delivering exceptional short-term results with limited resources. A condition for innovation is being enthusiastic and experimental, and being prepared to break with convention. This attitude will be one of the consequences of the successful executive performance transformation.

Finally, it is vital to acknowledge that the impact of Personal Leadership Excellence on your performance transformation goes well beyond business success. It allows you to be passionate and playful, engage with and inspire the people around you – at work and at home.

You will be able to make a unique and distinct difference in highly competitive business environments, be a role model for others, while experiencing a great sense of accomplishment, confidence and enjoyment. Ultimately, it will lead to a great and worthwhile life-experience.

For those of you who have already started your journey, or are about to embark on it, this should always be the aim. Not a quick fix or a short-lived change, but a thorough performance transformation that leads you to be consistently at your personal best. Make it happen – you deserve it!

ACKNOWLEDGEMENTS

I am very grateful to all the clients who have participated in the interviews for the research of this book. I am proud of you not only because of what you have achieved in your careers and personal journeys, but also because you have the greatness to share your lessons and with that, be an inspiration for others.

I would like to thank my wife Sabrina for your love and constant encouragement throughout my career, and your invaluable support in shaping this book. Your brilliant ability to jump from the big picture to the tiniest detail and back again is simply amazing.

Special thanks to Sven from my team for your creativity, ongoing support, involvement and dedication in providing valuable input for the book. And I particularly thank everyone who has provided additional feedback on the manuscript: Amit, Andrea, Dominique, Liz, and Tom.

And finally, many thanks to Matthew from Urbane Publications for your support and collaboration over the last years.

ABOUT THE AUTHOR

Dr. Christian Marcolli has worked with corporate executives, business leaders, market-leading brands and top athletes all around the world, helping them achieve incomparable, long-term success.

He is a world-class expert on sustainable high performance. In the media, his work has been described as, "an experience that will stay with you for life".

As the founder and CEO of Marcolli Executive Excellence, a specialized, boutique-style management consulting firm based in Switzerland, Christian supports a global roster of clients who are the market leaders of today – and tomorrow.

Since 1997, Christian works with hundreds of clients

each year, utilizing pioneering strategies and cutting-edge research aimed at helping individuals, teams and entire organizations around the globe accomplish peak performance. For several years, Christian was a guest lecturer at the Swiss Federal Institute of Technology (ETH) in Zurich, one of the world's leading universities.

MARCOLLI
EXECUTIVE
EXCELLENCE

www.marcolli.com

ABOUT MARCOLLI EXECUTIVE EXCELLENCE

Marcolli Executive Excellence is a highly specialized, boutique-style management consulting firm focused on fostering Personal Leadership Excellence, driving Team Excellence and creating Organizational Health.

Marcolli Executive Excellence has one specific objective:

Maximizing individual and team performance to lead organizations to their optimum capacity. Through its pioneering work, clients accomplish peak performance in their professional lives, resulting in incomparable long-term, sustainable success.

The services reach far beyond basic coaching and leadership development. It works closely with influential Executives, business leaders, corporate top talents, diverse business teams and entire organizations to develop the foundation for sustainable high performance. Offering more than two decades of experience and highly innovative models, it supports its clients, who are often already at the top of their fields, reach even greater heights.

If you would like to use the comprehensive *Executive Performance Melting Point Tool* to carefully identify your Melting Point in combination with the renowned Personal Leadership Excellence – P^{6}PROP® Profile for yourself, your leadership teams and/or your organization with the exclusive support of Dr. Christian Marcolli or one of his certified performance coaches, please visit: **www.marcolli.com**.

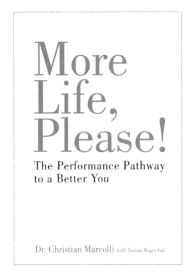

MORE LIFE, PLEASE!

Our life can be challenging. Is there time for a successful career AND those we love? We are driven by our successes, but often the most important moments are those we create with each other. We all strive to get more from life, but can struggle to find a positive harmonization between our career and family commitments. Business leaders and corporate performers constantly focus on achieving ambitious objectives – the next step, the next goal - and building positive lasting partnerships. But how can we bring those dynamic strengths into our private lives, far beyond the office desk into our homes?

Renowned performance expert, father, and husband Dr. Christian Marcolli successfully works with global business icons and Olympic gold medalists. His award-winning book *More Life, Please!* takes you from adequate to astounding in easy to follow and practical steps, changing your life for the better, and helping you engage more positively with everyone you interact with.

ISBN 978-1-909273-93-1, Urbane Publications

Urbane Publications is dedicated to developing new author voices, and publishing fiction and non-fiction that challenges, thrills and fascinates.
From page-turning novels to innovative reference books, our goal is to publish what YOU want to read.

Find out more at
urbanepublications.com